Beach at the Casino, Palm Beach, Fla.—68

Ocean Avenue, Palm Beach, Fla.

206,565. (J.V.)

The Breakers, Palm Beach, Florida.

THE BREAKERS

A CENTURY OF GRAND TRADITIONS

CHARLES LOCKWOOD

THE BREAKERS PALM BEACH, INC.

Second edition

ISBN 0-9649743-1-2

Printed in Singapore

Archetype Press and the
author are grateful for the
assistance of John Bradway,
Brie Suncine, Dale Carlson,
Shari Mantegna, James
Ponce, and the entire staff
of The Breakers. They
also wish to thank Sandra
Barghini, chief curator
of the Henry Morrison
Flagler Museum, and Ellen
Donovan, administrator
of the Historical Society
of Palm Beach County,
for their help with historic
photographs for the book.

Published by The Breakers Palm Beach, Inc.
One South County Road
Palm Beach, Florida 33480
561-655-6611
www.thebreakers.com

Paul N. Leone, President
David A. Burke, Vice President, Sales and Marketing
John Bradway, Director of Strategic Marketing
Brie Suncine, South Florida Advertising Manager

Produced by Archetype Press, Inc.
Diane Maddex, Project Director and Editor
Robert L. Wiser, Designer
Gretchen Smith Mui, Assistant Editor

Illustration Credits
Except for the following, all photographs are from The Breakers
Collection. Slim Aarons: back jacket flap. All World Vintage
Photos, Palm Beach: 16–17, 28 (top). Paul Berry: 38 (top). Bettmann
Archive: 38 (bottom). Lucien Capehart: 57 (top and bottom left).
Ed Chappell: 49. Sammy Todd Dyess: 4–5, 6–7, 65 (bottom right),
70–71, 74 (top), 75, 77 (top). Henry Fechtman: front jacket, 13,
54–55, 61, 86 (top), 93 (top). Henry Morrison Flagler Museum
Archives: first endpaper, 6 (top), 9, 19 (top), 20 (left), 22 (top and
bottom), 23 (top), 24–25 (top), 27 (right), 28–29 (bottom center and
right), 30 (bottom left), 30–31 (bottom center), 35 (left and bottom
right), 36 (bottom left), 36–37, 42–43, 51 (right), 63 (top right),
65 (top), 80 (top left and right), 81, third endpaper. Dan Forer: 48,
58. Hillwood Museum: 46 (top left). Historical Society of Palm
Beach County: second endpaper, 1, 2–3, 6 (center and bottom),
15 (right), 16 (left), 20–21, 22 (center), 23 (bottom), 24 (left), 24–25
(bottom), 26–27, 28 (bottom left), 29 (top), 30–31 (top), 31 (bottom
right), 32–33, 33 (bottom right), 35 (top right), 36 (top left), 43 (top
and bottom right), 44–45, 46 (bottom), 46–47 (top center), 47
(bottom), 62–63, 71 (right), 83 (right), fourth endpaper. Balthazar
Korab: 10–11, 14–15, 50–51, 52–53, 56, 60, 64, 66, 67, 80 bottom,
back jacket. Mary McCulley: 54 (left), 68 (top). Robert Nelson:
76 (bottom). Palm Beach Post, photo by Richard Graulich: 89 (top).
Michael Price: 53, 72 (bottom). Jerry Rabinowitz: 88 (bottom).
Greg Ross: 53 (right), 76 (top), 78. St. Augustine Historical
Society: 18 (bottom). Curtice Taylor (handtinting): 1, 2–3. Turner
Construction Company: 39 (bottom).

Front jacket: Arriving guests'
first view of The Breakers,
with its new brick driveway
and tropical floral displays.

Back jacket: The Atlantic's
breakers, seen through the
windows of the Circle.

First endpaper: The Cocoa-
nut Grove, located between
The Breakers and the Royal
Poinciana Hotel (now gone).

Second endpaper: Diving
at the first Beach Casino.

Page 1: The Beach Casino
of the Palm Beach Inn
(1896–1903), which was later
renamed The Breakers.

Pages 2–3: The second
Breakers (1904–25).

Pages 4–5: The third
Breakers, which opened
on December 29, 1926.

Page 6: Old postcards of
the beach, Pine Walk, and
the current Breakers.

Pages 10–11: The breakers
that gave the resort its name.

Third and fourth endpapers:
The old South Terrace,
now enclosed as the hotel's
Ponce de Leon Ballroom.

Foreword

Henry M. Flagler, whose portrait was painted in 1899 by R. Madrazo, visited Florida for the first time in 1878, when he was forty-eight years old. After scaling back his responsibilities with the Standard Oil Company, he began a new career: developing the "paradise" he found in Florida. One of his projects was The Breakers, which he built in 1896.

No story about The Breakers can begin without recognizing its founder, Henry Morrison Flagler, who was one of the great figures in American business history. Although not as well known as his partner, John D. Rockefeller, Flagler had just as much to do with the success of the original Standard Oil Company. These men virtually created a major industry. For all the criticism of the age of "robber barons," business people such as Flagler, Rockefeller, Andrew Carnegie and J. P. Morgan put America ahead to stay as an industrial power. This economic success led to an incredibly high standard of living for the American people, one that has long been a model for the rest of the world.

Flagler had a vision of Florida's potential as a winter resort, and from the 1880s until his death in 1913 he spent a good part of his Standard Oil fortune making his vision a reality. The Breakers is a famous part of the Flagler System of hotels, which ran from St. Augustine to Key West and tied into Flagler's Florida East Coast Railway.

Today The Breakers continues a long tradition in the hospitality business. We are proud of our history but also excited about the present and the future of this great resort. Guests can see our continued commitment to maintaining and enhancing a unique franchise, as well as constant efforts by our staff to provide first-class service. We are proud of the people associated with the hotel, all of whom work hard to make it a world-class resort. They are committed to excellence and have the energy and competence to achieve it.

This book is a story about the hotel's more than one hundred years of history. It is a tribute not only to Henry Flagler but also to all the people associated with The Breakers over the years—people such as William R. Kenan Jr., who with his two sisters provided the funds to build the present Breakers. I should also mention three men who followed William R. Kenan Jr. in managing the Flagler businesses: Frank H. Kenan, James G. Kenan, and Lawrence Lewis Jr. Frank H. Kenan served as chairman and chief executive during a critical period and provided the leadership and financial standards that helped fund several stages of renovation during the 1990s. This revised edition is dedicated to Owen G. Kenan, who passed away in 2002. As vice chairman beginning in 1986, Owen served a critical role in the redevelopment of The Breakers.

We hope that The Breakers will continue to be as special for our guests today and tomorrow as it has been in years past. This book tells a great history, but perhaps the best is yet to come.

James G. Kenan III
Chairman, Flagler System, Inc.

Contents

Introduction

In America only a handful of hotels and resorts can truly be called legends. The Breakers is one of these. Located in the exclusive island community of Palm Beach sixty-five miles north of Miami, The Breakers stands amid 140 acres of lush, tropical gardens, overlooking its half-mile-long private beach and the Atlantic Ocean. A sumptuous Italian Renaissance palace by the sea, it is modeled after the historic Villa Medici in Rome and encompasses splashing fountains, flower-filled courtyards, graceful arches and loggias, and twin belvedere towers.

The extraordinary history of The Breakers begins with the Standard Oil millionaire Henry Flagler, who opened Florida's east coast to development in the late nineteenth and early twentieth centuries. The first Breakers, which he built in 1896 as a winter resort named the Palm Beach Inn, was an immediate success, attracting the cream of American society. When it burned in 1903, Flagler built a second Breakers—larger and more luxurious—on the same commanding site. Opened in 1904, the rambling, colonial-style Breakers won widespread praise. In 1925, like its predecessor, the second Breakers burned in a spectacular fire. Although Flagler had died twelve years earlier, his heirs showed his same determination and vision. Within months, on the same oceanfront location, they began design and construction of the third Breakers—the splendid hotel that guests see today.

Now past the century mark, The Breakers celebrates its history while it looks to the future. Continual improvements, from a new Golf Clubhouse to a seaside Spa to a variety of modern dining experiences, offer guests the same first-class service envisioned by Flagler as the resort changes with the times. For the next century and beyond, The Breakers is committed to maintaining the look of a palace with the feel of an inn.

Opposite: The new red brick main drive, framed by swaying palm trees and colorful tropical flowers, heralds visitors' arrival at the Palm Beach landmark.

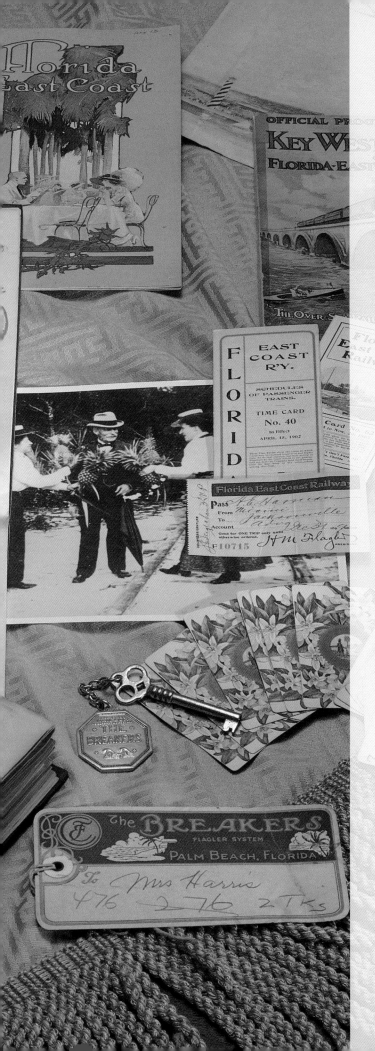

A Century of Grand Traditions

Above: Earlier in the century The Breakers' guests gathered at the second Beach Casino every morning by 11:00 a.m. A few changed into swimming clothes, but most simply "took the air."

Left: Henry Flagler and his Florida East Coast Railway Company transformed emerging communities into a tropical paradise—launching the state's role as a magnet for visitors.

Waiting for Change

Above: Sloops once plied Lake Worth near present-day Palm Beach, where cabbage palms and mastic trees provided shade for afternoon outings. Some early residents survived by salvaging lumber and scrap metal from ships that occasionally foundered on the offshore reefs.

Right: Except for its handful of towns and cities, one of Florida's most notable features in the 1880s was its watery swamps, usually explored only by hardy residents.

In the late nineteenth century Florida residents proudly boasted that St. Augustine, founded by the Spanish in 1565, was the oldest city in the United States. But Florida was also, they were reluctant to admit, the nation's most primitive state east of the Mississippi River.

Towns were scarce in Florida in 1880, and those that did exist—such as the coastal port cities of St. Augustine, Pensacola, Jacksonville, and Tampa—were small. According to that year's federal census, St. Augustine's population was 2,293, Pensacola's was 6,845, Jacksonville's was 7,650, and Tampa's was a mere 720. Key West, at the very tip of the state, was the largest settlement, with 16,000 persons.

The towns themselves were primitive by the standards of the day. True, historic St. Augustine was becoming a winter destination for northern travelers. But Joseph W. Howe, author of *Winter Homes for Invalids,* advised his readers to find their accommodations in a private home, not at a hotel or inn: "The old hotels in the town generally lack all the requisites of a healthy residence, and, unless they are improved, they should be shunned under all circumstances."

Growth and progress seemed decades away. Florida in 1880 was mostly swampland, grasslands, and scrub forest. Transportation was rudimentary, even in the more populous northern counties. Roads, where they existed, were little more than narrow, rutted, muddy paths. Only five hundred miles of railroads served the entire state.

Lake Worth, Palm Beach, and Hypoluxo, isolated settlements along the shores of the twenty-two-mile-long Lake Worth, each had a population of only several dozen residents. Most houses were little more than shacks with roofs of palm fronds, and the hardy residents survived by farming, hunting, fishing, and beachcombing. Regular postal service was not established until 1880. But the rustic island community would soon enter an era of revolutionary change that would transform it and the entire state.

A Century of Grand Traditions

Flagler Discovers Florida

Opposite, top: The 450-room, Moorish-style Ponce de Leon Hotel, designed by Carrère and Hastings, opened in St. Augustine on January 10, 1888. Once the world's largest concrete structure, it has been preserved as Flagler College.

Opposite, bottom: The Alcazar, a 325-room hotel also designed by Carrère and Hastings, was Flagler's second hotel in St. Augustine and shared the same land-scaped park with the Ponce de Leon. The Alcazar now serves as the city hall and Lightner Museum.

Right, top: In 1870, at age forty, Flagler became a partner in John D. Rockefeller's Standard Oil Company and first traveled to Florida eight years later. He once claimed that he could make more in a week on Wall Street than a year buying Florida real estate and building hotels.

Right, bottom: Flagler began collecting art and fine furnishings, first for his homes and then for his Florida hotels. The Sultan's Favorite (1886), by Giminez Martin, was originally at the Ponce de Leon Hotel in St. Augustine but today hangs across from The Breakers' Venetian Ballroom.

Henry Flagler, the son of a Presbyterian minister, was born on January 2, 1830, in Hopewell, New York. Through innate business acumen, sweeping vision, and boundless energy, he accumulated a vast fortune in Cleveland and New York as a partner of John D. Rockefeller in the Standard Oil Company. When the Standard Oil Trust was founded in 1882, Flagler, then only fifty-two years old, could depend on an annual income of several million dollars from dividends, and he gradually withdrew from the company's day-to-day operations. He then turned his talents to a new role: resort developer and railroad king.

Flagler first visited Florida in March 1878, when he brought his ailing wife, the former Mary Harkness, to Jacksonville to enjoy the mild weather after the frigid northern winter. Following her death in 1881 from tuberculosis and his remarriage, he visited St. Augustine in February 1885. There he acquired the site of his Ponce de Leon Hotel, Florida's first luxury hotel. In 1889 he opened the Alcazar Hotel across the street and purchased a nearby 200-room hotel, which he renamed the Cordova.

St. Augustine could not contain a man of Flagler's ambition. He started buying and building Florida railroads, rapidly extending the lines down the state's east coast. As these regions were opened to development and tourism, Flagler acquired or constructed more hotels along the coast, starting with the Hotel Ormond near Daytona Beach.

In 1893 Flagler announced one of his boldest plans: to extend his rail line south to isolated Lake Worth and construct the Royal Poinciana Hotel on its eastern shore. This transformation of a semitropical backwater would become one of his—and Florida's—greatest triumphs.

"I am spending an unnecessary amount of money in the foundation walls, but I comfort myself with the reflection that a hundred years hence ... [the Ponce de Leon Hotel will be] better, because of my extravagance."

Henry Flagler, Letter to Franklin W. Smith, December 26, 1885

Following the Crowd

Right: The Royal Poinciana's guests initially rode a ferry across Lake Worth from the West Palm Beach railroad station. In 1896 Flagler built a bridge so that trains could come virtually to the front door. Some guests traveled in their own rail cars—the ultimate luxury.

Above: Invitations to the elegant balls held at the Royal Poinciana Hotel were always coveted. Favorites included gala New Year's Eve parties like this one in 1909 as well as the traditional George Washington's Birthday Ball held to honor the president each February.

When the Royal Poinciana opened on Lake Worth on February 11, 1894, it created a sensation. The six-story, Georgian-style hotel had 540 rooms, an impressive lobby and rotunda, an immense dining room, vast kitchens, three elevators, and electricity in every room. Its 140-acre grounds, which stretched from the Atlantic Ocean to Lake Worth, initially included a yacht club on the lake, the Cocoanut Grove near the hotel, and a beach club (known as the Beach Casino) overlooking the ocean. From opening day the Royal Poinciana attracted well-to-do, socially prominent guests, including the Vanderbilt family, the closest thing to royalty in late-nineteenth-century America. Their patronage ensured the hotel's success.

The Royal Poinciana's several-month-long "season" began in mid-December. Guests would board trains in frosty northern and midwestern cities and arrive in balmy Palm Beach several days later. During the first two seasons the train stopped in West Palm Beach, where guests took a ferry across Lake Worth to the hotel. In March 1896 Flagler completed a bridge so that trains delivered guests directly to Palm Beach and the Royal Poinciana.

Soon after the opening of its second season, Flagler announced that the Royal Poinciana had more guests than any other south Florida hotel, a startling accomplishment considering that Palm Beach was still the end of the line of the Florida East Coast Railway. Certainly the town itself—with its several dozen shacks and cottages, two stores, and a few inns—held little allure for wealthy travelers apart from its pleasant climate and natural beauty. The only reason people came to Palm Beach was to stay at the Royal Poinciana. Flagler had built the destination, provided easy access on his railroad, and the elite of American society crowded into this tiny town as if at his command.

One day in New York, Flagler met Henry Bradley Plant, who was building resorts and railroads on Florida's west coast. "Friend Flagler," Plant reportedly asked, "where is that place you call Palm Beach?"

"Friend Plant," Flagler replied, "just follow the crowd."

Down by The Breakers

"Palm Beach possesses an indefinable charm, with the bluest of blue skies, the delicious, balmy air, the tropical foliage, and the translucent water of lake and ocean."

The Tatler, 1902

Opposite: Flagler's Georgian Revival–style Palm Beach Inn along the ocean eventually became so popular that it eclipsed the Royal Poinciana Hotel and had to be expanded several times.

Right, top: A group of early guests at the Palm Beach Inn gathered on the steps for an informal photograph.

Right, center: Wicker pedicycles became a Palm Beach institution that allowed visitors to sightsee in comfort.

Right, bottom: The 1,000-foot-long pier served the ships of Flagler's P and O Steamship Line.

From its opening in 1894, the Royal Poinciana proved so popular that over the next decade Flagler continually expanded the hotel and improved its grounds. He built tennis courts, croquet lawns, bicycle paths, clay-pigeon shooting ranges, a saltwater swimming pool, a nine-hole golf course, and a small marina for the launches and sailboats that took guests onto Lake Worth and the Atlantic Ocean. "There is no resort hotel in the country more popular than this has been since its first season, a popularity growing with each year," announced *The Tatler*, a fashionable magazine, on January 20, 1900.

Eventually, the Royal Poinciana became the world's largest wooden hotel, stretching more than 1,800 feet along Lake Worth. Its 1,100 rooms accommodated 1,750 guests. The H-shaped dining room was so large that it could seat 1,700 diners at one time. The hallways were so extensive—more than three miles in length—that bellhops sometimes delivered messages and packages from the front desk to guest rooms by bicycle.

Delighted that many of America's richest and most socially prominent families shared his love for Palm Beach and sensing another business opportunity, Flagler developed a second hotel—the Palm Beach Inn—on the beachfront portion of the Royal Poinciana's property. The inn, an expansion of an existing house, opened on January 16, 1896, and was fully booked for most of that season because it was smaller and quieter than the vast Royal Poinciana and because it was right on the shore of the Atlantic Ocean. "This charming hotel grows upon its guests each day," declared *The Tatler* on February 4, 1899. "The bright sunny rooms, broad verandahs, the dash and flow of the ocean, its constant ebb and flow, alike delight the visitor."

Many regular Palm Beach guests shared *The Tatler's* enthusiasm for Flagler's newest hotel. So they asked for rooms not at the Royal Poinciana but "down by the breakers." The name stuck. When Flagler doubled the size of the Palm Beach Inn for the 1901 season, he renamed it The Breakers.

A Day in Palm Beach

By the turn of the century small, isolated Palm Beach, which received its name in 1886, had become one of the world's best-known winter resorts. The palm frond–roofed shacks of the 1880s were rapidly giving way to handsome cottages and occasional mansions. According to Baedeker's authoritative *United States: Handbook for Travelers* for 1909, Palm Beach "ranks as one of the most fashionable winter-resorts of the United States, and in some respects rivals the resorts of the Mediterranean." To many Americans, Palm Beach was simply the "Queen of the Winter Resorts."

Guests at The Breakers and Royal Poinciana were fully occupied during their stays of several weeks to several months. According to Cleveland Amory in *The Last Resorts*, visitors followed a daily routine. After breakfast many rode the mule car to the bathing pavilion, enjoyed refresh-

ments, or changed into their full-length swimming clothes and relaxed on the beach. At 1:00 p.m. they gathered for a lunch of several courses, followed by a little dancing. In the afternoon guests strolled through the gardens, went for rides along Lake Worth, toured nearby pineapple plantations and orange groves, or visited Alligator Joe's wild animal farm, where they could see local species such as turtles and manatees or watch Joe "wrestle" alligators.

At 5:00 p.m. the vacationers recuperated by taking tea in the famed Cocoanut Grove, where Dabney's orchestra played the latest hits. At 7:45 p.m. guests returned to the hotel to change for dinner, probably their fifth or sixth wardrobe change of the day. Dinner was served at 8:00 p.m., followed by more dancing in the Cocoanut Grove. Then the pleasantly tired visitors retired for the night.

Opposite, top left: Alligator Joe wrestled alligators and displayed manatees where the Everglades Club now stands.

Left: Visitors who chose not to walk could ride in comfort on the mule car.

Below: The enlarged Breakers had ocean views for almost everyone. A few hardy guests actually walked along the beach or went swimming in the afternoon.

Fame and Misfortune

Flagler seemed to be sitting on top of the world. He happily claimed credit for Palm Beach's extraordinary rise to fame. "While I agree with you in the belief that Palm Beach 'has come to stay'," he remarked in 1903, "it is, I think, an undisputed fact that my investments have given it its permanence as a winter resort." Flagler successfully extended the Florida East Coast Railway to Miami in 1896 and opened the Royal Palm Hotel on Biscayne Bay for the 1897 season. He built the Hotel Colonial in Nassau, the Bahamas. Most boldly, he planned to extend his railroad all the way to Key West.

Flagler probably relished the challenge of developing Florida's east coast. After the deaths of his first wife, Mary, in 1881 and his daughter Jennie Louise in 1889, he may have also sought an escape from grief and a measure of immortality. Another daughter, Carrie, had died in childhood; his only surviving child was his son, Harry.

In June 1883 Flagler had married Ida Alice Shrouds, Mary's nurse-companion during her final illness. Ida later suffered from delusions and in 1897 was committed to an institution for the insane. Four years afterward they received a divorce. On August 24, 1901, Flagler married Mary Lily Kenan of North Carolina. As a wedding present Flagler built her a white marble mansion named Whitehall near the Royal Poinciana. Completed in 1902, the fifty-five-room mansion was designed by Carrère and Hastings, the architects of the Ponce de Leon and Alcazar Hotels and, in 1926, the Standard Oil Building in New York City. In his personal life as well as his professional life, Flagler had attained a high point of contentment.

Then, as Flagler settled into his new marriage and palatial home, tragedy struck. On June 9, 1903, as workers were enlarging the wooden building for the fourth time in less than a decade, The Breakers burned down.

The seventy-three-year-old Flagler was shocked by the loss of his favorite hotel but definitely not beaten. Two weeks later he announced that The Breakers would not only be rebuilt but also would open for the upcoming winter season. "We are going to try to make a feature of The Breakers," he vowed, "and if possible, make it better than the Poinciana."

Above: Mary Lily Kenan became Flagler's third wife in August 1901. A year later the couple moved into Whitehall, their new home near The Breakers.

Left: Fire ravaged The Breakers on June 9, 1903. Although guests managed to rescue most of their belongings and hotel employees saved some of the furniture, the building was a complete loss. Flagler boldly declared that he would build another Breakers on the same site.

Back in Business

Above: Guests included the Hearsts in 1924. Opposite, top: William K. Vanderbilt Jr. (left) and his wife (seated) posed in 1907 with Leland Sterry, The Breakers' manager; Lawrence Waterbury; and Fred Sterry, the Royal Poinciana Hotel's manager.

Flagler made good on his promise. On February 1, 1904, The Breakers reopened to universal acclaim. According to the American novelist Henry James, who visited in 1905, the hotel was "vast and cool and fair, friendly, breezy, shiny, swabbed and burnished like a royal yacht, really immaculate and delightful."

The new Breakers, a rambling four-story, colonial-style building constructed entirely of wood, contained 425 rooms and suites. Other than its sheer size and expensively appointed lobby and public rooms, the hotel's most notable architectural features were its extensive porches and verandahs overlooking the ocean and grounds. Rooms started at $4 a night, including three meals a day.

The Breakers' guest register, like its predecessor's, read like a "who's who" of early-twentieth-century America: various Rockefellers, Vanderbilts, and Astors; the tycoons Andrew Carnegie and J. P. Morgan; the publisher William Randolph Hearst and his family; the five-and-dime kings W. T. Grant and J. C. Penney; and even assorted European nobility and U.S. presidents.

These privileged guests typically arrived in Palm Beach on their own private railroad car or yacht. If they desired even more space and privacy than they would have enjoyed in a luxurious ocean-view suite, they stayed in one of ten special cottages along the beach.

Overleaf, top: The ten elegant Breakers cottages— shingled, New England–style structures with names such as Ocean View, Surf, Wave Crest, Seaside, and Nautilus—came complete with full hotel services and ample servant quarters.

Overleaf, bottom: Guests passed their days by relaxing at the beach, strolling the gardens, or scouting for shells. If they were not interested in physical activity, they could hire a pedicycle for an outing.

Below: When it came to fun, The Breakers offered something for everyone. Postcards captured period bathing costumes, a 1916 Golf and Tennis Ball, and the popular Beach Casino.

BATHING BEACH, BREAKERS HOTEL, PALM BEACH, FLA.

BREAKERS HOTEL, PALM BEACH, FLA.

Bathing Casino, Palm Beach, Fla.

THE BREAKERS

View of Hotel Breakers from Ocean Pier,
Palm Beach, Fla.

"The Breakers," Palm Beach

A Century of Grand Traditions

COTTAGES FROM THE PIER, PALM BEACH, FLORIDA.

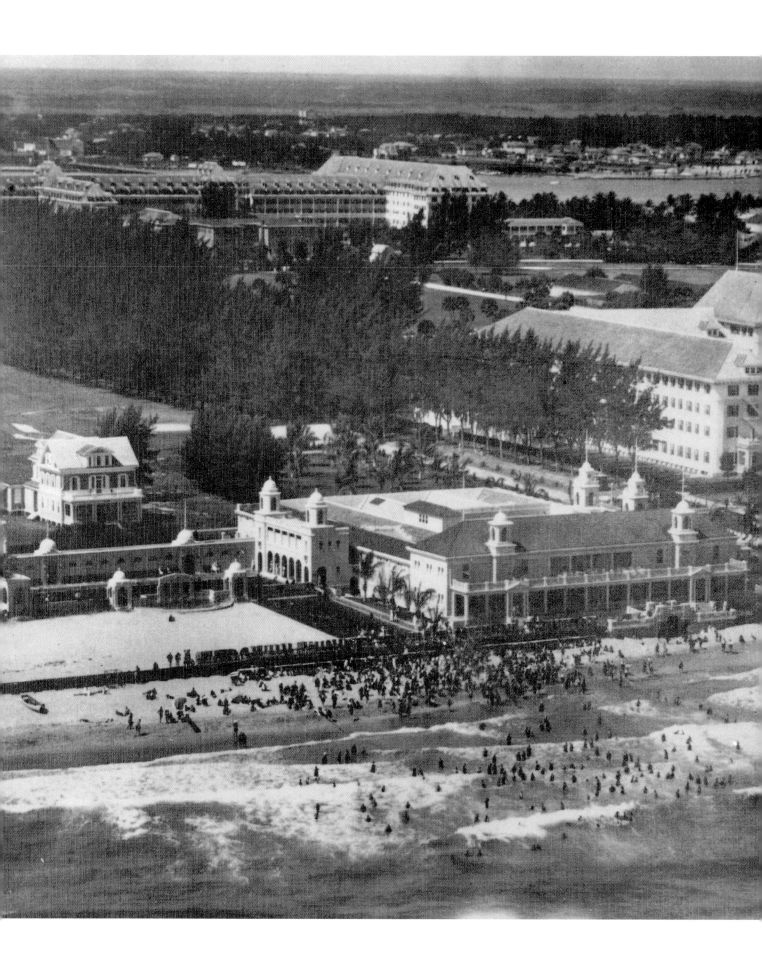

A Century of Grand Traditions

Fun in the Sun

In his quest to make the new Breakers the consummate winter resort for the nation's social and financial elite, Flagler continuously improved his already magnificent hotel and expanded its outdoor recreation and sporting facilities.

Golf was the most popular sport among hotel guests. The Breakers thus hired some of the nation's best golfers to manage its eighteen-hole golf course and hosted a half dozen tournaments during January and February.

To please the many yachtsmen at The Breakers, Flagler, who owned four yachts, helped found the Lake Worth Yacht Club and provided a building for its clubhouse. He also served as president of the Motorboat and Carnival Association, which held a yearly regatta on Lake Worth.

Along the beach just south of the hotel, Flagler built a new, Mediterranean-style Beach Casino with extensive locker rooms, refreshment facilities, a saltwater swimming pool, and a lovely portico overlooking the beach and sea. "A long pier extending into the ocean," reported Baedeker's 1909 guide, "affords opportunities for fishing."

In keeping with turn-of-the-century proprieties, the strict social rules governing the endless rounds of teas, dinners, and dances inside The Breakers extended to all the hotel's outdoor recreation and sporting activities as well. Gentlemen never would have thought of playing golf unless they wore a jacket and tie. Ladies sported head-to-toe bathing attire on the beach. Nothing was allowed to disturb the graciousness, beauty, and exclusivity of The Breakers and thus its appeal to its elite guests.

Left: By the early 1900s many of America's richest families flocked to Palm Beach, staying at the new Breakers (right) and the Royal Poinciana (background) overlooking Lake Worth. On the beach is The Breakers' second Beach Casino. A brochure for Flagler's Florida East Coast Railway boasted: "No hotel on the Florida East Coast is better appointed or more popular than The Breakers."

Below: Although some were more brazen, women staying at The Breakers were discouraged from exposing their "limbs" (few dared use the terms "arms" and "legs" in polite society). A hotel attendant stood outside the ladies' locker room at the Beach Casino to make sure that every guest observed the rules of propriety.

The Eighth Wonder of the World

In 1910 Henry Flagler was eighty years old. Many of his friends and business colleagues had long since retired or died, but Flagler, although troubled by worsening deafness, insisted on fulfilling his vision for Florida. He pursued his boldest business venture yet—the extension of his Florida East Coast Railway from Miami to Key West.

The Key West Extension, begun in May 1905, was a Herculean endeavor. The first fifty miles of track, south of Miami, were built through the alligator-infested Everglades, while its remaining 106 miles jumped from island to island before reaching Key West. Between islands Flagler's construction crews had to create a solid roadbed of rubble and stone for the rail line or construct massive concrete viaducts and bridges, many several miles long.

This construction project faced enormous obstacles. All the food and water for several thousand workers had to be delivered by train. Mosquitoes were relentless. Many workers suffered from heat and sickness. Bad weather, including hurricanes, damaged partly completed viaducts and bridges and disrupted work schedules.

These challenges hindered but did not thwart Flagler. On January 22, 1912, the eighty-two-year-old tycoon arrived in Key West aboard his private railroad car for the official opening of the Key West Extension. The cheering crowd included the governor, congressional representatives, senators, and foreign ambassadors. This new railroad, more than one speaker boasted, was "the eighth wonder of the world." Flagler's empire now extended along the entire east coast of this once-primitive state.

A little more than a year after fulfilling his vision, Flagler died at his cottage, the Nautilus, near The Breakers, after suffering a fall at Whitehall. He was buried in St. Augustine in the Flagler family mausoleum at Memorial Presbyterian Church, which he had built more than twenty years earlier. Flagler's vast Florida legacy was well cared for. Mary Lily Flagler inherited most of his estate, and on her death in 1917 most of the Flagler empire passed down to her family, the Kenans of North Carolina and the Lewises of Virginia.

Above: Henry Flagler, photographed in 1907, was not shy about his success. After he invited President William McKinley to come to Florida in 1898, Flagler remarked, "My domain begins at Jacksonville." Once his railway was extended to Key West, travelers could make the previously difficult trip south from Miami in both comfort and style.

"The journey is much like a trip at sea, with the Gulf of Mexico on one side and the Straits of Florida on the other. The terminus will be at Key West."

Baedeker's *United States: Handbook for Travelers,* 1909

Opposite, left: Flagler's Florida East Coast Railway and his resort hotels opened the state's once-isolated east coast to development. This map shows Flagler's impact in 1926, thirteen years after his death in Palm Beach.

Opposite, top right: The first of Flagler's trains to arrive in Key West in 1912 was met by a huge crowd and a color guard. In 1935 a Labor Day hurricane destroyed the Key West Extension, which was later rebuilt by the government as the Overseas Highway.

Opposite, bottom right: The Flaglers traveled on their own railroad car.

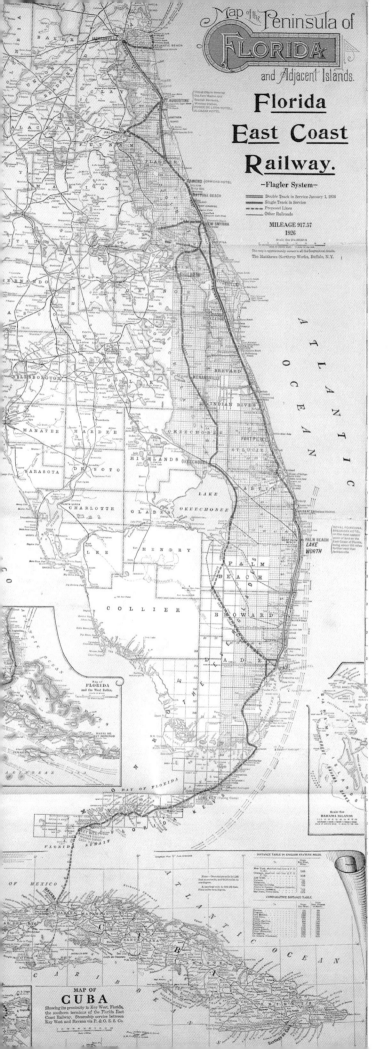

"Fire in the South Wing!"

Above: From its sumptuous lobby to the boardwalk, The Breakers was the place to be as the 1920s dawned.

Right: The unthinkable happened again in 1925. A fast-moving fire destroyed the second Breakers, providing a frightening spectacle for visitors as the wooden structure quickly burned.

In the 1910s and 1920s Flagler's beloved Palm Beach was the world-renowned playground of the rich and elite. Many millionaires stayed at The Breakers for the season. Others built lavish Spanish haciendas nearby, often following designs by the architect Addison Mizner. Exclusive shops, restaurants, and clubs filled the once-sleepy town. Expensive motorcars cruised the palm-lined streets. "Everything about Palm Beach in the 1920s was superlative," one observer noted. "Everything was solid gold, extra large, outsized, the most expensive, the most ostentatious, and the most opulent."

But on March 18, 1925, tragedy again struck the Flagler empire. That afternoon the cry "Fire in the south wing!" suddenly filled The Breakers. "Everyone in town turned out either to fight the fire or to watch the effort to put out the blaze," reported one eyewitness. "All around the hotel, the grounds were strewn with mink coats and steamer trunks that had been thrown from the windows."

Despite the firefighters' efforts, The Breakers was doomed. Strong southeast winds fanned the fire. The palatial hotel, built almost entirely of wood, was soon engulfed in flames. The billowing clouds of dark smoke that poured out of the hotel could be seen twenty miles away.

Fortunately, no lives were lost at The Breakers, a miracle considering the number of guests and employees. But something grand and beautiful had died. By evening all that remained of America's leading resort hotel were several brick chimneys rising out of the smoldering ashes.

Flagler's heirs refused to be cowed by this catastrophe. Led by William R. Kenan Jr., president of both the Florida East Coast Hotel Company and the Florida East Coast Railway Company and the brother of Mary Lily Flagler, they showed the same determination and vision as Flagler himself. Shortly after the fire the Florida East Coast Hotel Company announced that it would build the world's finest resort hotel on the site of The Breakers and do so in time for the opening of the 1926–27 winter season, little more than a year away.

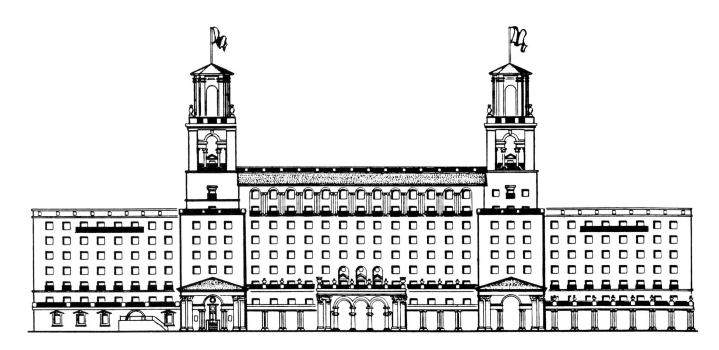

A Century of Grand Traditions

A Phoenix from the Ashes

*Opposite: The architectural
inspiration for the new
Breakers was the Villa
Medici in Rome, a
Renaissance landmark.*

*Right, top: William R.
Kenan Jr., president of the
Florida East Coast Hotel
Company (center), led the
effort to produce a palatial
new hotel in record time.*

*Right, bottom: The architect
Leonard Schultze modeled
the front fountain on one in
Florence's Boboli Gardens.*

The new Breakers, declared the hotel's builders, would be "the acme of perfection in design and magnificence ... nothing was to be omitted that could in any way add to the comfort of the prominent guests who each year were accustomed to spend a considerable part of the season at Palm Beach."

For the new hotel's architects the company selected the firm of Schultze and Weaver, which later designed the fabled Waldorf-Astoria, Pierre, and Sherry Netherlands Hotels in New York City. William R. Kenan Jr. knew Schultze and Weaver's work because he lived in a luxurious Park Avenue building designed by the architects.

For the hotel's architectural style Schultze and Weaver selected the Italian Renaissance. Historical revivalism was the fashion in the 1920s, and Americans were busy constructing Gothic-inspired skyscrapers, Spanish-style houses, and Parisian-inspired shops. During an earlier trip to Rome, Leonard Schultze had admired the twin-towered Villa Medici (circa 1575), and he used that building as the basis for The Breakers' facade.

The third Breakers was the commission of a lifetime. In a matter of months Schultze and Weaver not only planned The Breakers' new building but also designed or selected all the furnishings, down to the linens, china, and silverware. The firm additionally planned the fountains, gardens, and landscaping around the hotel.

Schultze and Weaver ensured that the new Breakers would be fireproof and able to withstand the hurricanes that periodically hit the Florida coast. The hotel was to be built of reinforced concrete, strengthened by 1,100 tons of reinforced steel.

On December 4, 1925, the New York City–based Turner Construction Company signed a contract to rebuild The Breakers. Construction began in January 1926. The seven-story hotel had to be built, furnished, and landscaped to open just after Christmas 1926, the start of the Palm Beach season. The race was on.

Racing against the Clock

Above: Hundreds of photographs were taken of The Breakers during its construction. The Turner Construction Company dedicated itself to making the new hotel "absolutely fireproof" and able to withstand Florida's hurricanes.

Opposite: The twin towers quickly became Palm Beach landmarks, while oceanfront wings reached out to surround the central courtyard and Grand Loggia. When construction was complete, the ocean side presented a regal face to the sea.

"The Breakers would open on time," L. S. Homer, Turner Construction Company's superintendent for The Breakers, recalled afterwards, "if not a day was wasted, if every one of the thousands of different items of materials entering into the structure arrived on time, if there was no shortage of labor, if there was no delay in transportation of materials, if the weather held fairly good, and many other 'ifs.'" In its New York headquarters the company created a separate department to manage construction of The Breakers. The manufacture of material by various subcontractors throughout the county and the shipment of this material to the construction site was closely supervised.

To facilitate deliveries, a railroad line was built directly to the construction and storage yards in front of the rapidly rising hotel. More than 1,300 carloads of material went into the hotel proper: 492 carloads of stone, 191 of brick and tile for exterior and interior walls, 190 of cement, 144 of lumber, and 89 of plaster and artificial stone.

More than 1,200 construction workers labored on The Breakers seven days a week, including nights. They were fed in a large mess hall and housed in dormitory ships or in tents on the grounds. Seventy-two artisans were brought from Italy to complete the Renaissance-style paintings on the lobby and first-floor public room ceilings.

Excitement about the new Breakers reached such a pitch by early December that the hotel's management barred all curiosity seekers from the nearly finished hotel. "This move was necessary," reported the *Palm Beach Post-Times*, "because so many persons were anxious to see how far the building had progressed that work was impeded." By mid-December workers were arranging tables and chairs in the handsome Florentine Dining Room and unpacking carloads of furniture for the 425 guest rooms. The $7 million Breakers would open, as planned, on December 29, 1926. The Florida East Coast Hotel Company, Schultze and Weaver, and Turner Construction Company had won the biggest race of their careers.

"At the time the contract was let the construction conditions in Florida were at their worst. Everywhere large hotels and other projets were being rushed to completion to accommodate the winter influx of tourists for 1925–1926. All jobs were being run at night and on Sundays.... In many instances money lost its power as a medium of exchange and materials were bartered for as of old."

L. S. Homer, Turner Construction Company

A Century of Grand Traditions

"A Milestone in Perfection"

Devoted patrons of the previous Breakers eagerly awaited the new hotel's opening. Would the new Italian Renaissance–style hotel live up to their expectations? Would it claim its predecessors' mantle as America's consummate winter resort hotel? Several days before the hotel opened vacationers began arriving in Palm Beach, hoping to be among the first to move into the new landmark.

The Breakers exceeded everyone's expectations. When the first guests arrived at the hotel on the morning of December 29, 1926, they were thrilled at their first sight of the seven-story Renaissance palazzo rising at the end of an allée lined by palm trees. But more awaited these usually jaded guests: the Main Lobby, with its arched ceiling decorated with paintings; the vast Florentine Dining Room, with its richly decorated, beamed ceiling in the Florentine style; the sun-filled North and South Loggias; and the shaded terraces and landscaped patios.

The Breakers had a total of 425 guest rooms, of which fifty were suites with separate living rooms. Most rooms faced the ocean, and many suites had private porches or balconies. The hotel also included fifty "well-furnished" rooms for servants traveling with guests.

The Breakers offered its patrons a fine selection of shops, including Cosmos Fertiti's barber shop, Mme. Selma McCann's "hairdressing parlor," Greenleaf and Crosby jewelry, Madam Mogabgab gowns, Madam Scaaf lingerie and linens, Neilds flowers and confections, Anthony haberdashery and shoes, Michalyean oriental carpets and antique furniture, and Elizabeth Eagleston gifts and antiques. Guests could even monitor their stock and bond portfolios without leaving the premises, for E. F. Hutton maintained its Palm Beach office at the hotel.

The Breakers won praise from vacationers and Palm Beach residents alike. According to the May 1927 *Architectural Forum*, The Breakers was "without doubt one of the most magnificent and successful examples of a palatial winter resort hotel." On December 30, 1926, the *Palm Beach Post-Times* was more effusive: "The new Breakers is a milestone in the architectural perfection of American hotels."

Above: Guest rooms and baths in the new hotel were luxurious for the times.

Left: Visitors jostled with each other to be the first to sign the new Breakers' guest register each year.

Overleaf: Kermit Roosevelt (foreground), Theodore Roosevelt's son, joined the seaside promenade in 1927.

The Breakers Goes to War

With the crash of the stock market in 1929, the Roaring Twenties gave way to the somber Depression years of the 1930s. Palm Beach escaped the worst of this worldwide financial catastrophe. "Palm Beach itself remained intact," observed *Fortune* in 1936. "Its frequenters, so far as they lost anything, lost little. And that little they seem now to have regained, as Palm Beach draws near the height of another season." As many of the nation's once-renowned resort hotels (including the antiquated, hurricane-damaged Royal Poinciana) closed their doors forever, The Breakers continued to attract its affluent clientele and earned a profit throughout much of the 1930s. At the height of the season a double room (including three meals) was $22 to $40 a day, while suites, with meals, cost up to $50 a day—astronomical sums in that period.

But even Palm Beach and The Breakers could not fend off the world forever. War clouds were gathering in Europe and Asia during the late 1930s. After the United States entered the war in December 1941, German U-boats

torpedoed more than a dozen Allied vessels in the shipping lanes off the Florida coast.

The Breakers also went to war. The hotel became the U.S. Army's Ream General Hospital on September 10, 1942. "Once Temple of Luxury, Breakers Hotel Is Now Quiet Haven for Heroes," declared the *Palm Beach Post-Times*. Thousands of servicemen and women convalesced at The Breakers. As the soldiers recuperated, many marveled at the grandeur of their hospital. "We were in awe of the place, because it was so beautiful," one Coast Guard officer recalled years later.

In mid-1944, as the war was drawing to a close, the U.S. Army returned The Breakers to the Florida East Coast Hotel Company. The hotel was immediately restored to its earlier glory, and by mid-December 1944 it was ready to receive its first guests in more than two years. But the world had changed dramatically since The Breakers had opened its doors in 1926. Was there a place in the postwar world for this reminder of a quieter, more elegant past?

Opposite, top left: The cereal heiress Marjorie Merriweather Post, owner of Mar-a-Lago, frequently attended balls and social events at The Breakers.

Left: Beachfront cabanas were just as popular in 1934 as they are today.

Opposite, bottom: After the hotel served as a hospital in World War II, the staff returned in December 1944.

Below: Servicemen and women enjoyed the sun and amenities at The Breakers.

Rebirth of a Legend

When guests returned to The Breakers on Christmas Eve 1944, their historic hotel seemed unchanged. Even some faces were the same, because many staff members had returned to their jobs.

Yet The Breakers, like other legendary hotels across the country, was affected by changes in Americans' lifestyles. During the 1950s and 1960s many longtime guests began vacationing at the resort for just several weeks rather than for the entire winter season. By the 1970s and 1980s guests often made visits of only a few days. Corporations and organizations began holding meetings, retreats, and conventions at hotels. In addition, Palm Beach was becoming a year-round destination, not just a winter resort.

The Breakers expanded in the 1960s and, after it was fully air conditioned in 1970, remained open year-round. Added facilities included a new golf clubhouse, the Venetian Ballroom facing the sea wall, extensive meeting spaces, and 150 new guest rooms. In 1973 The Breakers was added to the National Register of Historic Places, joining America's most important architectural and historic landmarks.

In the years before and after its centennial in 1996, the resort underwent a thorough revitalization to meet twenty-first-century needs while respecting its celebrated history. Guest rooms, enlarged and redesigned, now number 560, including fifty-seven suites. The top two floors house the Flagler Club, a concierge level featuring luxurious accommodations, the private Flagler Club Terrace, and the Flagler Club Lounge. Along the ocean a 20,000-square-foot Spa and a Mediterranean-style beach club await guests. Golfers' beloved Ocean Course—the state's oldest—has been reconfigured to meet the needs of today's skilled players, complete with a new golf and tennis clubhouse recalling Florida's past. An oceanfront conference center and the new Ponce de Leon Ballroom welcome visitors, and a multitude of dining options cater to every taste.

Restoration of the historic architectural features of The Breakers—such as the ceiling paintings in the Main Lobby, the Circle, the Florentine Room, the Magnolia Room, the Gold Room, and the Mediterranean Ballroom—has been an important part of the renovations carried out. In keeping with the hotel's Italian Renaissance style, the Main Lobby was also refurbished. Outside, new walkways and landscaping designed to entice adults and children of all ages have turned The Breakers into a modern garden paradise.

"The inspiration for the building, and especially for many of the chief rooms of the main floor, was frankly derived from different well known examples of Italian palace architecture.... One is impressed with the consistency and unity of the whole composition and the admirable way in which the body of precedent has been intelligently adapted...."

The Architectural Forum,
May 1927

Opposite: Between arched windows looking onto the Mediterranean Courtyard and steps leading up to the Florentine Room, the hotel's North Loggia offers a restful place for a brief hideaway under a coffered ceiling containing painted panels. The new decor was designed by Frank Nicholson Inc.

Above: Mixing the instincts of a detective with the skills of an artist, a chemist, and a historian, conservators researched the hotel's original painted ceilings and authentically restored them. Paintings in the Circle were done on canvas strips and then affixed to the ceiling.

A Palace by the Sea

Above: Since 1926 The Breakers' guests have begun their visits under the distinguished arches of its porte-cochère—the first of many architectural marvels to be found at the hotel.

Left: The historic building captures the spirit of the Italian Renaissance outside and in. A colonnaded loggia south of the entrance provides shade and a spot to watch a game of croquet.

Florida Renaissance

Rising seven stories into the blue Florida sky, with its twin towers soaring even higher, The Breakers draws the eye from miles around, even from distant Interstate 95. The architectural glories of this "palace by the sea" range from its aristocratic Italian Renaissance style and pleasing scale and proportions to its exquisite decorative details.

At the end of the 1,000-foot-long main drive leading to The Breakers—lined with 100 matching royal and Canary Island date palms framing carpetlike medians bursting with blooms—visitors arrive beneath the hotel's impressive porte-cochère. Framed by a set of triple arches, this two-story Renaissance porch is crowned with a balustrade accented with an urn at each corner. A large fountain, modeled after a well-known example in the Boboli Gardens (1549–88) in Florence, dominates the center of the landscaped plaza. Water splashes from the small uppermost bowl into a larger, beautifully sculpted bowl below, supported by four water nymphs representing the four seasons. The water then cascades into the still-larger octagonal basin at the base, surrounded by broad travertine steps. At night the fountain is lighted, offering a welcoming beacon to guests returning to the hotel.

The buff-colored stucco facade is modeled on the Villa Medici in Rome but on the far larger scale required for a vast resort hotel. Its towers rise 175 feet to the flagpoles, and the west facade is 450 feet long. The receiving yard and service entrance are hidden behind walls and landscaping north of the porte-cochère. The serene Palm Court and its shaded loggia (sun porch), which overlook the gardens and golf course, are just south of the entrance.

In keeping with the overall Italian Renaissance style of The Breakers, the hotel's facades are a delightful mixture of ground-level loggias and patios, balustraded terraces and stairways, a variety of neoclassical decorative accents, and balustrade-topped rooflines of red tile. The facade and familiar belvedere towers, however, are merely hints of the splendors found inside The Breakers.

Above: Generations of guests have been photographed below the distinctive towers of The Breakers.

Left: Beyond the front fountain are colorful flower beds, the triple-arched porte-cochère, and the hotel's elegant Italian Renaissance facade. The drive was recently paved with 200,000 antique clay bricks and landscaped with tropical plantings.

The Main Lobby

Inspired by the Great Hall of the Palazzo Carega (circa 1560) in Genoa, the Main Lobby is a spectacle of rich materials and decorations, stretching 200 feet parallel to the sea. Six two-story, Renaissance-arched windows look onto the tropically landscaped Mediterranean Courtyard. Under a custom handmade carpet, the floor is pink Tennessee marble with a Botticino marble base.

The lobby's pièce de résistance is its glorious barrel-vaulted plaster ceiling, embellished with paintings of flora and fauna, gods and goddesses, and free-form decorations. The walls are a cream-colored precast travertine, hung with paintings and three of the hotel's eight heirloom tapestries. Children play in "Les Enfants Jardiniers," a nine-by-ten-foot silk and wool tapestry, while companion pieces tell the stories of Achilles and Telemachus. Historical legends are depicted in the other tapestries throughout the hotel.

The story behind the tapestries is as fascinating as the textiles themselves. Dr. Owen Kenan, a first cousin of Mary Lily Flagler who was the doctor appointed by Henry Flagler to look after hotel guests during the winter season, purchased them for an extensive art collection housed at his apartment in Paris. When World War I threatened, Dr. Kenan became determined to travel to France to reclaim his treasures. Disregarding warnings from family and friends, he booked passage on the *Lusitania* in 1915. The ship foundered after being hit by a German torpedo, killing 1,198 passengers. Dr. Kenan was traveling with Alfred Vanderbilt, whose valet handed him a life jacket. Vanderbilt and his valet went down with the ship, but Dr. Kenan was rescued. His valuable collection was shipped to the Kenan family home in North Carolina, eventually given to the Henry Morrison Flagler Museum, and placed in The Breakers in the 1960s.

Recent restoration has given the tapestry collection new life. Each one was gently lowered from the walls with pulleys and rope and then wrapped. Textile conservators undertook the delicate task of wet cleaning, reinforcing, stitching, and securing them to ameliorate the effects of time, light, and the ocean air.

Above: Arriving guests are greeted at the front entrance by the hotel's bell staff—who are happy to offer a ride into the hotel's Main Lobby.

Right: The lobby's ceiling paintings, created in 1926 to recall a Renaissance villa, were restored by an expert team over three years. The conservators used ultraviolet light and microscopes to match the original materials and bring them back to life.

A Palace by the Sea

Opposite and top left: "Les Enfants Jardiniers," a silk and wool tapestry in the south lobby, dates from the early eighteenth century. Four carefree children play in this summertime scene. Two of them bounce on a seesaw, while one rides a stick horse. Flowers and musical instruments line the border of the hotel's most popular tapestry.

Below: Dr. Owen Kenan, Mary Lily Flagler's cousin, collected the colorful tapestries in France.

Left: Light, air, and the effects of aging necessitated a recent restoration of the hotel's eight historic tapestries. Textile conservators from the Biltmore Estate in Asheville, North Carolina, traveled to The Breakers to direct this effort. They photographed and catalogued the tapestries and then cleaned and reinforced them for the next century.

The Florentine Room

When The Breakers reopened in late December 1926, the Florentine Dining Room served all the guests' meals in two seatings, each capable of accommodating up to 550 diners. Guests were assigned a specific table for the duration of their stay, and the same waiter (who worked seven days a week in season) served them breakfast and lunch, another dinner—getting to know each guest's likes and dislikes.

Even today the historic space, home now to the award-winning L'Escalier at the Florentine Room, is one of the hotel's most memorable architectural spaces. Raised above the North Loggia by a flight of stone steps, the dining room looks out on the Mediterranean Courtyard. Accented by oak wainscoting, its walls are a creamy stone designed to look like travertine. Several dozen freestanding limestone columns support the magnificent eighteen-foot-high ceiling, which is embellished with massive beams and elaborate painted decorations, modeled after the four-teenth-century Palazzo Davanzati in Florence. Huge Venetian-style chandeliers illuminate the impressive 40-by-150-foot room.

Guests ascend six steps to reach L'Escalier, whose name (French for "staircase") connotes an elevated French cuisine many steps above the ordinary as well as exceptional service designed to heighten the dining experience. This award-winning, world-class dining destination, the hotel's flagship restaurant, features a theater-style exhibition kitchen. Among the chefs' favorite offerings are compli-mentary morsels to begin the meal called *amuse-bouches*, a foie gras de jour, a *menu de dégustation* of from six to eight courses, and a fromagier cart to finish.

Wines to accompany each meal come from the elegant Wine Cellar adjacent to L'Escalier, a customized display housing the hotel's renowned assemblage of wines. Nine-teenth-century European leaded glass fills the arched front, which leads to redwood racks on a floor featuring a vine-yard pattern engraved in Chinese slate. The cellar's wines are not just for dinner, however: during one Christmas week, a 1955 Chateau Latour was sent upstairs by room service at 3 a.m. to polish off a steak sandwich in style.

At the western end of the Florentine Room is the liv-ing room–style Tapestry Bar. Above a vintage mahogany bar constructed from a mantel in London's Caxton Hall, its 14-by-12-foot tapestry depicts "The Abdication of Charles V in 1555"—a palatial spot for tea or a cocktail.

Opposite: The Florentine Room's ceiling was cleverly designed to recall in plaster the time-worn wooden ceilings of Renaissance-era houses. Guests once dined in a "celebrity aisle" along the wall, so christened to make tables located away from the entrance more desirable. Today this dining area can be reserved for intimate dinners seating as many as sixteen guests.

Right, top: Flemish tapestries lend a regal, residential air to the living room–style Tapestry Bar.

Right, bottom: A solid redwood racking system, specially created for the Wine Cellar, houses 7,300 bottles of wine, representing some 1,250 varieties. Each year the cellar earns Wine Spectator's Grand Award.

The Circle

Few people realize that the Circle was an afterthought. When the management of The Breakers and architects Schultze and Weaver were designing the hotel in 1925 and 1926, they assumed that the vast Florentine Room would be large enough to accommodate the dining needs of all the guests. They were wrong.

As soon as The Breakers opened in December 1926, Palm Beach residents and visitors from other hotels flocked to the Florentine Room. Even two seatings could not handle the crowds, and The Breakers was forced to limit reservations to its own patrons. The managers assumed that the hotel's novelty would wear off by the start of the second season and that the crowds of outsiders would diminish. Again they were wrong. Schultze and Weaver came back to design a second dining room.

The Circle, which opened in late December 1928, is a large, two-story circular room with fifteen tall windows overlooking the North Lawn and the Atlantic Ocean. Seating up to four hundred guests, it quickly became one of the favored places to eat at The Breakers, a distinction it holds to this day. Its extravagent breakfast buffet and Sunday brunch have become Palm Beach traditions, and the Circle is in high demand for weddings and parties.

The room retains its original Renaissance-inspired decorative detail. The cream-colored walls are accented with marble trim, walnut woodwork, mirrors, and sconces. The thirty-foot ceiling is a shallow dome with eight oval murals depicting Renaissance landscapes such as the Villa Medici in Fiesole, outside Florence, and the famous Tivoli Gardens near Rome. These are accented by smaller panels of mythological characters. At the center of the dome a large Venetian crystal chandelier hangs from a stylized gold-leaf sunburst.

If visitors look carefully at the top of the south wall, just below the dome, they will spy a musicians' gallery, complete with a delicately carved balustrade. During some meals in the 1920s and 1930s, a chamber music ensemble would serenade diners from this balcony. But regular hotel guests knew that this gallery, before the repeal of Prohibition in 1933, was a private dining room unofficially known as The Breakers Club, where "members" could imbibe forbidden alcoholic beverages in privacy.

Left: The Florida East Coast Hotel Company owned and managed all of Henry Flagler's hotels, including The Breakers. This white-and-gold plate proudly carries the company's FEC logo.

Opposite: To accommodate the overflow guests from the Florentine Room, Leonard Schultze was asked to design a truly special room that would not be considered a second-class place to eat. Rising to this challenge, Schultze gave the 1928 dining room a variety of notable features, including its dramatic circular shape, a shallow dome with a skylight, elaborate wall paintings and decorations, and dramatic arched windows that look out to sea.

A Palace by the Sea

Left: The Circle has always been
one of the most photographed rooms
at The Breakers. A semicircle of
early waitresses mirrored the
dramatic shape of the room itself.
Behind them, the balustraded
musicians' gallery above the room
provided an elevated vantage point
as well as a hideaway for "members"
to have a drink during Prohibition.

Top: The room was added in 1928,
just two years after the hotel was
completed. Its signature domed
skylight survived the destructive
hurricane of 1928, which delayed
but did not stop the work.

Above: Like a sunburst, the ceiling
showers the dining room with
natural light drawn from outside.

The Ballrooms

Each year The Breakers hosts several hundred events in its ballrooms. Some are black-tie fund-raisers for charities such as the Heart Ball, the American Cancer Society Ball, and the March of Dimes Gala. The Red Cross Ball—Palm Beach's premier social event—has been held for three decades in the oceanfront Venetian Room. Counting hospital and university benefits, these events add millions of dollars each year to charitable coffers.

The 52-by-118-foot Mediterranean Ballroom, facing the Mediterranean Courtyard, is one of the most famous ballrooms in America. Modeled after the loggias of Italian villas, this magnificent room was originally the hotel's Grand Loggia and boasts elaborate ceiling paintings of the sky, large Venetian-style chandeliers, and tall, arched windows. An identical set of windows on the east side that once overlooked the ocean has been replaced by richly decorated doors leading to the Venetian Ballroom, an 80-by-120-foot space added in 1969. A recent $5 million renovation makes the 26-foot-high space glow even brighter with new windows, chandeliers, fabrics, and golden tones. While the Mediterranean Ballroom welcomes up to 600 persons, the Venetian accommodates as many as 1,400.

The latest addition is the Ponce de Leon Ballroom, a 15,000-square-foot space that is part of the resort's new oceanfront conference center; it can hold 1,200 persons for lunch or 800 ball goers. A new glass-covered limestone walk serves as an elegant porte-cochère for the ballroom. Nearby a brick promenade leads down to the ocean lawn.

So handsome, according to *Town and Country*, that "they require little more decoration than flowers, place cards, and celebrities," the ballrooms at The Breakers also host anniversary parties, bar mitzvahs, receptions for companies and organizations—and weddings. With its seaside location and wide range of amenities, the resort offers a special destination for those seeking a romantic place to take their vows. The design studio provides the floral arrangements and the decor, the catering service dishes up a restaurant experience, the building supplies the history, and all the bride and groom have to do is get to the hotel on time.

"It is said that more money has been raised for charity in The Breakers' capacious ballrooms than anyplace else in the world."

Town and Country,
March 1991

*Left and opposite, top:
In keeping with the hotel's
Italian Renaissance style,
the Mediterranean Ballroom
features decorative wall
paintings on spandrels above
cast-concrete Doric columns.*

*Opposite, bottom left:
Florida's explorer Juan Ponce
de Leon is remembered in
a spacious new ballroom
named for him in 1999.*

*Opposite, bottom right:
Offering exceptional views of
the Atlantic Ocean, the
Venetian Ballroom's windows
are fitted with custom coverings that complement the
room's fabric walls. Six
sparkling chandeliers show
off the cove ceiling's gold trim.*

The Gold and Magnolia Rooms

*Opposite: From its grand
fireplace to the painted
portraits and golden ceiling,
the Gold Room resembles an
early Renaissance chamber.*

*Right, top: Juan Ponce de
Leon, explorer of Florida,
is one of the notable faces
in the portrait niches.*

*Right, center: Rows of
golden cherubs in the deeply
incised plaster ceiling give
the Gold Room its name.*

*Right, bottom: The Mag-
nolia Room's plaster ceiling
is executed in softer tones
that recall the ceiling in the
adjacent Florentine Room.*

The impressive public rooms, loggias, and promenades of The Breakers attracted widespread comment when the hotel was completed in 1926. To justify the expense of such lavishly decorated first-floor public spaces, several observers noted at the time, a hotel typically required twice as many guest rooms. The public rooms were large as well as richly embellished. "One cannot fail to be impressed favorably by The Breakers' bigness, and the spacious breadth and dignity of scale everywhere evident," wrote *The Architectural Forum* in 1927.

The Gold Room, originally the South Lounge and now used for meetings, private functions, and weddings, is a replica of a room in Venice's Galleria Accademia. Its fireplace and overmantel—representing the Old and New Worlds—are elaborately carved, but its most impressive feature is the complex, diagonally paneled plaster ceiling.

The raised ornament is covered with gold leaf. Niches just below the ceiling contain portraits of Renaissance rulers and explorers of the New World. The paintings were executed by Alfred D. Crimi (1900–94), the son of a stonemason in Messina, Sicily. Over one summer in his New York studio, Crimi handpainted the images of the forty-four leaders, including Columbus and Ponce de Leon. He never saw them installed at The Breakers.

Framing the side door are an Aubusson tapestry showing a fisherman, "Le Cerf-Volant" (circa 1770), and a Flemish example picturing a music lesson, "Scene de Festin et Leçon de Musique" (circa 1700). The broken-pedimented doorway was originally hung with portières.

The Magnolia Room, which was once the living room–style North Lounge and is now also used for meetings and functions, was based on a gallery in a Roman palazzo. Nearly fifty feet square, like the Gold Room, this room features a Venetian-style stone fireplace and a richly decorated plaster ceiling. Above the fireplace hangs a tapestry, "Russian Games," showing eight characters playing blind man's bluff.

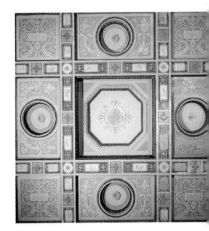

Courtyards and Terraces

One of greatest delights of The Breakers is its abundance of inviting open spaces. Courtyards, loggias, terraces, and promenades tempt guests out into the warm ocean breezes to enjoy the lovely views of the Atlantic, palm trees, and tropical flowers. After walking through the Mediterranean Courtyard at the center of the hotel, reading in the Palm Court, strolling along the ocean promenade, or enjoying a cool drink high up on the sixth-floor terrace of the Flagler Club, most would agree with Henry Flagler, who reported that he had discovered "a veritable Paradise."

A wide balustraded terrace leads visitors from the Main Lobby to the Mediterranean Courtyard to view its exotic flora under the open sky. Reflecting the hotel's Italian Renaissance inspiration, it was designed to provide sunshine as well as cross-ventilation for many rooms in the days before air conditioning. Commanding the center spot is a sunken, lily-filled reflecting pool with a fountain as its centerpiece.

At the front of the hotel, the Palm Court serves as an outdoor retreat where guests can relax and gaze across the croquet lawn to the newly landscaped grounds and tropical gardens. For vacationers who like to shop in addition to enjoying the outdoors, boutiques have been carefully fitted behind the court's arched passages.

Left: The hotel's arcaded boutiques recall the Old World ambience of the "vias," or shopping arcades, on Worth Avenue in Palm Beach. The stores offer fine crystal, jewelry, fragrances, gifts, gourmet foods, and clothing for young and old.

Opposite: The Palm Court is one of many open-air spaces that allow guests to savor tropical flowers and breezes—and to enjoy their purchases from the surrounding boutiques.

Below: Framed by classical balustrades, lined by walkways, and furnished with tropical flora, the hotel's serene Mediterranean Courtyard is a lush haven.

A Palace by the Sea

A Veritable Paradise

Above: Golf has been a hit at The Breakers ever since Henry Flagler opened the Ocean Course in 1897. Today the tropical greens are Florida's most historic eighteen-hole golf course.

Left: The links of the Ocean Course wind their way through 140 luxurious acres. Its new clubhouse, located in view of the hotel, conveys a residential look with airy wraparound porches.

Gardens and Groves

As guests travel up the lush allée of palms that leads to the hotel's porte-cochère, it becomes obvious that they have entered "a vast semi-tropical paradise," as the 1909 Baedeker's reported. While The Breakers staff works hard to get guests into their rooms, new landscaping has been "designed to entice them back outdoors," explains Danny Miller, the director of golf and grounds, who brought about the new focus on the outside of the resort.

The verdant 140-acre grounds—the last open land in the heart of Palm Beach—offer a remarkable variety of landscape experiences: theme gardens, traditional floral plantings, semitropical shrubs and trees, and the much-loved Ocean Course for golfers, with its shimmering ponds. Outdoor rooms, announced with arched entryways, invite exploration and appeal to all the senses: graduated hues in a rainbow garden attract one's vision, floral scents perfume the air, fragrant herbs pique the taste buds. Respecting different guest activities, the main entrance drive is painted in bright colors, the quiet corners and patios of The Breakers in more muted hues for relaxation.

The hundred species of annuals in the 10,000-square-foot Color Garden Walk are chosen not just for their unique tones but also for their hardiness in the salty sea air. The Tropical Garden near Pine Walk harnesses exotic Florida bromeliads, cycads, and palms. Close by the Family Entertainment Center is a treat for young guests: a Secret Garden secluded within a 1,200-foot maze and filled with flowers chosen to attract colorful butterflies. Every botanical specimen in the vast canvas of the resort's landscape has a purpose.

The Breakers offers its guests a weekly tour of the extensive grounds, during which they see some of the 34,000 annuals (planted three times a year) and more than 3,000 palm trees, all surrounded by five miles of formal hedges. More than forty groundskeepers are usually at work, planting, trimming, mowing the acres of lawns and golf course, and continually adding palms to keep the "palm" in Palm Beach.

"The grounds are filled with bearing cocoanut-trees, palms of many varieties, and countless foliage and flowring plants and shrubs...."

Baedeker's *United States: Handbook for Travelers*, 1909

Left, top: The Color Garden Walk was designed to stimulate the senses of sight and smell and offer a place for contemplation. One of many awards received for the new landscaping was given for the best use of color.

Left, center: Gardenias in the Tropical Garden Walk are clearly marked for guests.

Left, bottom: Changing flower displays add bursts of color, including the red, white, and blue hues of the flag.

Opposite: Hiding out in the Children's Secret Garden, which features a maze of hedges, is no problem at all.

A Veritable Paradise

The Ocean Course

The oldest eighteen-hole golf course in Florida, the Ocean Course at The Breakers has been transformed into championship greens ready to meet the twenty-first century as a great golf destination. Opened originally in 1897 alongside the first Breakers building, the course was designed by Alexander H. Findlay, a native of Scotland, who laid out courses for Henry Flagler's oceanfront resorts from St. Augustine to Miami. At the turn of the twentieth century it had sand greens and totaled only 4,925 yards. In the 1920s the renowned Donald Ross remodeled Findlay's course, converting the greens to grass and increasing its length. By then jackets were no longer required on warm days, but guests had to wear their best clothes in the clubhouse.

Changes in the early 1990s made the 70-par course more challenging and scenic. And then in 2000, under the direction of the famed golf course architect Brian Silva, the 90 acres of antique links were carefully renovated to add new elevated putting surfaces and deeply recessed bunkers, state-of-the-art turf grass from tee to green, and 200 additional yards of play length, all surrounded by stone aggregate cart paths, palms, and flowering tropical trees and brushed by ocean breezes. (Golfers never see the same display of annual flowers on the course more than once.) With random bunkers and fairways that weave between sandy hazards, the deceptively difficult 6,167-yard Ocean Course retains the feel of other vintage courses. Underneath its historic greens, however, lies a high-tech system for irrigation and drainage.

The course's Old World design extends to its new centerpiece: the 35,000-square-foot golf and tennis clubhouse (ten lighted Har-Tru courts are next door). Ringed by galleries, the clapboard-and-shingle structure is reminiscent of an old Florida estate. A pro shop and spacious locker rooms are downstairs, while a popular restaurant with an outdoor dining veranda awaits above. The Flagler Steakhouse serves the finest USDA prime-grade steaks and chops for hotel guests, club members, and local residents who play more than 32,000 rounds a year here. Hotel guests may also try out a private golf course at Breakers West—just beginning its own first century.

Above: A bridge near the new clubhouse was built with sandstone found on the site.

Opposite: The Ocean Course, framed here by the second Breakers (1904–25), has welcomed presidents, world leaders, and celebrities, as well as golf legends.

Right, top and bottom: From the lobby to the Flagler Steakhouse, the clubhouse is designed for comfort.

The Beach Club and Spa

"Outdoor life at The Breakers is one continual source of health and enjoyment," declared an advertisement for the hotel not long after it opened. Early Breakers guests played golf and tennis, swam in the ocean or the pool at the bathing pavilion, fished off the now-vanished ocean pier, bicycled around the grounds, played croquet, or yachted on Lake Worth and the Atlantic Ocean. Today The Breakers is a one-of-a-kind resort where guests can pursue an even wider range of recreation and relaxation. When they are not hitting a golf or tennis ball, the place to be is the brand-new Beach Club and Spa overlooking the ocean shoreline.

Built in a refined Mediterranean style on a broad oceanfront deck, the complex encompasses four pools—the main swimming pool, kept at a comfortable eighty-three degrees; a children's pool; a three-lane, 25-meter lap pool; and a beachside pool—as well as cabanas offering the ultimate in beachfront privacy; the 20,000-square-foot Spa; the Beach Club Restaurant with outdoor seating and a 6,000-square-foot rooftop terrace above it; a patio bar and the Reef Bar; and, to make exercise more palatable, a fitness center whose 14-foot windows offer a view of the Atlantic Ocean across a closely tended lawn. And not least, down where the breakers still roll in: the one-half mile of private beach.

After the sandy shore, one of the most popular areas is the indoor-outdoor Spa at The Breakers. Inside, fragrant facial treatments and relaxing massages are offered for women and men too in seventeen rooms and suites plus a beauty salon, all embracing a tropically landscaped courtyard. Active guests can choose a workout in the lap pool, Jacuzzi, fitness center, or upper terrace.

Young and old visitors enjoy a multitude of other sports and recreational activities at The Breakers: from beach volleyball to water aerobics and from nature walks to bicycling, not to mention golf and tennis, and, of course, a game of croquet. The croquet lawn adjacent to the main entrance of The Breakers—the oldest croquet facility in the United States—hosts the Palm Beach Croquet Club Invitational, the oldest continuously held tournament in the United States.

Left, top: The arches of the Beach Club Restaurant, located just beyond the main pool, convey a Mediterranean aura reminiscent of the original architectural style of The Breakers.

Left, bottom: Relaxing poolside remains one of visitors' favorite activities.

Opposite, top: Surrounded by water—four pools and the ocean—an Italianate tower marks the location for fun and relaxation at The Breakers Beach Club.

Opposite, bottom: Tai chi and other fitness exercises get the day off to an energetic start sixty feet above the sea atop the Ocean Terrace.

A Veritable Paradise 77

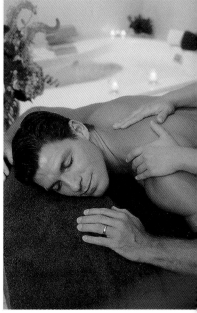

Above: Spa services include massages from Shiatsu and sports massage to aroma-therapy and reflexology.

Left: The secluded courtyard that marks the entrance to the Spa at The Breakers offers a restful interlude in a day that may begin with a hydrating facial and end with a tropical citrus body wrap. Behind the spa's philosophy is a belief that "purifying the soul begins with cleansing the body."

Opposite: A day at the Spa can include laps in the pool just outside the entrance.

Pine Walk

A stroll along Pine Walk, a long row of Australian pines, transports visitors to a tropical rain forest resounding with the calls of brilliantly plumed parrots and their winged cousins. As the result of a parrot craze a generation ago, thousands of parrots, cockatoos, and macaws were imported into the United States. Many of these birds later escaped from homes and bird breeders. Lucky ones found their way to the grounds of The Breakers.

Conditions at the hotel are ideal for such parrots of Central and South America as Rinsch's Amazons, Yellow Napes, Mexican Redheads, Orange Wings, and Blue Fronts. The palm trees, Australian pines, and other tropical vegetation provide the necessary food and shelter. The birds feed on the buds of the pine trees as well as tropical fruits. The pines also have sheltering cavities that offer good nesting spots and protect the birds at night from owls, one of their natural predators. Under these near-perfect conditions The Breakers' parrots have thrived, multiplied, and often interbred, producing ever-more colorful and exotic subspecies.

Pine Walk leads to Whitehall, the grand home on Lake Worth that Henry Flagler built for his third wife, Mary Lily, to celebrate their marriage in 1901. Designed in the Beaux-Arts style, it boasts a 40-by-110-foot entrance hall with Louis XIV furniture and a monumental staircase, an Italian Renaissance library, a Louis XIV music room, a Louis XV ballroom, an Elizabethan-style breakfast room, a Francis I dining room, a Louis XVI salon, a master suite, and fourteen guest bedrooms. The dinners, parties, and balls that the Flaglers gave at Whitehall were legendary.

In the 1920s new owners built a hotel behind Whitehall. By 1959 the mansion was in danger of being demolished. Acting quickly, Jean Flagler Matthews, the daughter of Henry Flagler's son, Harry, formed a foundation that purchased the property and has since restored the mansion as a historic house museum dedicated to educating the public about America's Gilded Age and the life of Henry Flagler.

Above: Mary Lily Flagler's portrait, painted in 1902 by Marietta Cotton, hangs in the music room at Whitehall, the Flaglers' home.

Left, top: After the Flaglers moved into Whitehall in 1902, they hosted large parties that were the talk of Palm Beach. Sometimes, all this socializing was tiring for Flagler, who turned eighty in 1910. He then quietly left the parties, using a secret staircase to reach his second-floor bedroom without being noticed by the guests.

Left, bottom, and opposite: Pine Walk, seen today and in the early 1900s, connects The Breakers and Whitehall, which is now the Henry Morrison Flagler Museum.

A Day in the Life of The Breakers

Above: Although clothing styles have changed, Palm Beach visitors have enjoyed bicycling around the town since the resort was first developed by Henry Flagler in the 1890s.

Left: A solitary swim in the lap pool outside the beach club- house gets the day off to a healthful start. Endless choices await: golf, tennis, shopping, reading on the beach—or bicycling.

2:00 p.m. "Good afternoon. Welcome to The Breakers."

Greeting you in the porte-cochère, the doorman loads your luggage onto the bellman's cart. Then he directs you through the front door to the marble reception desk in the lobby. "Have a pleasant stay," he adds. Guests playing croquet and flying kites on the front lawn already are.

The Breakers is a metropolis in miniature, offering 560 rooms, including fifty-seven suites. On a typical day several hundred guests check in and out of this oceanfront city. Several thousand people dine in its eight restaurants, play golf on its two courses, attend meetings in the twenty-five meeting rooms, and dance at black-tie galas in the Mediterranean, Venetian, and Ponce de Leon Ballrooms. With 1,800 employees, it is a large business enterprise, independently owned and managed by Flagler System, Inc.

But what goes on behind the scenes? How does a hotel like The Breakers operate day and night, playing its many roles simultaneously and seemingly effortlessly?

2:15 p.m. You arrive in your room and quickly walk to the window to gaze at the Atlantic Ocean. Around you is everything to make your room feel even better than home, from a comfortable bed with down pillows and a CD alarm clock to a bathroom stocked with fluffy towels, fragrant amenities, and white terrycloth bathrobes. The living area has an oversized armoire with a color television, not to mention dual telephone lines with voice mail and a data port in each phone, high-speed Internet access, Playstation video games, and in-room movies.

2:30 p.m. A few luncheon guests are still lingering over dessert in the restaurants, but the dinner crews have already arrived in the kitchens, ready to display their talents to the fullest. The executive chef gives the cooks the forecasted number of meals to be prepared that night. The estimate is based on current reservations plus a calculated forecast about last-minute reservations and walk-ins, factoring in the day of the week, the time of year, and any special events occurring at the hotel. The hot-side crew begins to prepare sauces and stocks and sets up its stations. The cold-side crew starts dicing vegetables and making decorative garnishes for the plates. The pastry chef works on pear almond tarts and warm cheese dumplings.

3:00 p.m. A dozen hotel guests and three visitors from Palm Beach gather in the South Loggia, admiring this richly decorated space and gazing out onto the Mediterranean

Courtyard beyond. Hotel historian James Ponce arrives promptly and recounts the story of Henry Flagler's development of Florida and The Breakers. They are immediately beguiled by the hotel's history and follow him for the next hour for a visit through the hotel's most significant public rooms and areas—as well as back in time.

4:00 p.m. The telephone rings constantly at the concierge desk in the Main Lobby. The hotel concierges are asked some questions over and over again: What is the best way to sightsee? How can I make restaurant reservations in Palm Beach? What about shopping along Worth Avenue? They arrange a tee time for one guest and, miraculously, find a choice restaurant table for four at 7 p.m. for another.

The concierges also welcome unusual and challenging requests. A woman attending a wedding at The Breakers did not want to leave the hotel to buy a new dress. The concierge thus went to Worth Avenue and brought back five dresses to her suite. She purchased three.

Another guest who experienced car trouble as she drove from the west coast of Florida to The Breakers called the concierge, who immediately dispatched a limousine at her request. After the guest had arrived and settled into her room, she phoned the concierge again. "I'd like you to buy me a new Cadillac. Dark blue exterior. Beige leather interior." The concierge called a local dealer, who located the exact model and colors. When the concierge phoned the guest with the good news and quoted the asking price, she said, "Tell him to take $5,000 off the price, and I'll write the check today." Before the day was over, the concierge had delivered the car to the grateful guest at the hotel's main entrance.

5:00 p.m. A traditional game of croquet is starting on the croquet lawn, just south of the main entrance. Regulation croquet at The Breakers (instruction provided) is a world away from the familiar "smash and laugh" games at home. The mallets are longer and heavier; the wickets are narrower and more challenging. If requested, a waiter might set up a serving table alongside the court and pour champagne and mineral water. The proper accompaniment? Hors d'oeuvres served from a silver tray.

Left: Children visiting The Breakers can choose from a roster of activities just for them, from tennis lessons to snorkeling and Coconut Crew Camp. Or they can fly a kite on the front lawn.

5:15 p.m. The hotel entrance is thronged with guests returning from an afternoon of shopping or sightseeing in Palm Beach. Other visitors are arriving for a reception in the Mediterranean Courtyard. Businesspeople are leaving conferences. Palm Beach residents come for drinks at the Tapestry Bar. The doormen remain unfazed by the commotion. All day long they direct traffic, making sure that the cars, SUVs, taxis, and limousines do not block the main entrance. On a busy day in season the valet parking attendants handle a thousand cars, and up to five thousand persons walk through the front door of The Breakers. The doormen also serve as combination tour guides and concierges, answering all sorts of questions from guests.

5:30 p.m. The Seafood Bar is already serving fresh clams and oysters, crab cakes, and creamy chowders. Although dinner at L'Escalier and the Italian Restaurant is yet to begin, their kitchens are busy too. Cooks set up the various preparation lines, work on dishes requiring long lead times, and put sauces and stocks on the steam tables. About this time the restaurant chefs show the dinner crew and then the dining room staff the evening's specials— perhaps an appetizer of soft-shell crab and an entrée of rack of lamb with eggplant caviar. Afterward they go through the line, double-checking to make sure that everything meets their exacting standards.

6:00 p.m. Turndown attendants start the evening service. For the next four hours each one will enter approximately forty empty guest rooms, turn down the bed, leave fresh towels and chocolates, and, if necessary, tidy up the bathroom. Just before leaving, the attendant puts a compact disc in the CD player to welcome returning guests with the sleep-inducing sound of the ocean.

6:30 p.m. L'Escalier has opened for dinner, and the tables begin to fill with guests who may spend two or three hours enjoying their meals and luxuriating in one of the most exquisite dining spaces in America. A theater-style kitchen turns the evening into a culinary exhibition. Many diners are staying at The Breakers and eat in one of the resort's restaurants every night. Others are nearby

Clockwise from top left: Memorable food fuels The Breakers, from pasta in the Italian Restaurant to an intimate prenuptial dinner at L'Escalier in the Florentine Room, to the chefs' gourmet show, to fruits de mer *in the oceanside Seafood Bar.*

residents who have come to The Breakers to celebrate a special event. To all it is a destination, not just a hotel.

7:00 p.m. A candlelight wedding is just getting under way in the Mediterranean Courtyard, whose Old World architecture creates a fairytale setting. The couple's family and friends have gathered here from across the country to turn the nuptials into a winter vacation of several days. Ever since she was a girl, the bride had dreamed of saying "I do" at The Breakers, and the hotel took care of everything: the rehearsal dinner, the ceremony, the reception in the Circle, entertainment, photography, videography, and flowers. The groom spent the afternoon on the Ocean Course, while the bride and her mother enjoyed a day of total bliss at the Spa. On the morning after, the newlyweds plan to return for a couples massage along the oceanfront.

7:30 p.m. The first guests for a gala charity ball begin arriving. Most men are wearing black tie. The women are more dazzling: many are dressed in full-length, formal evening gowns and wear sparkling jewels. They stroll through the lobby, walk down the South Loggia, which is lined with flags and marines in dress blues, and enter the Gold Room, where they pass through the receiving line. Next they go across the hall into the Mediterranean Ballroom for cocktails. As a string quartet plays, photographers busily snap pictures of the celebrities. Just before 9:00 p.m. a banquet waiter dressed in a tuxedo and white gloves walks around the Mediterranean Ballroom, subtly ringing chimes as the row of double doors opens to the Venetian Ballroom. Guests enter the brilliantly lighted room and find their places at the circular tables arranged around the edges of the dance floor. The marine color guard forms a double line down the middle of the room, and several marines escort the event's leaders to the head table. Foreign dignitaries receive the same honors. As the waiters begin to serve the appetizers, the orchestra starts its first number, and eager couples head to the dance floor. The gala ball has begun.

9:00 p.m. The cooks have reached the height of their evening activity. Waiters keep bringing in late dinner orders at all the restaurants, while under the Ponce de Leon Ballroom the banquet kitchen is preparing meals for seventy-five guests attending a surprise birthday party in the Magnolia Room; at the same time, several hundred entrées and desserts are being plated for the gala ball. And orders for room service dinners keep streaming in.

11:00 p.m. By now the last dinner guests have usually left L'Escalier and the Flagler Steakhouse, and the Tapestry Bar is closing. The birthday party in the Magnolia Room is over. On the outdoor terrace of the Flagler Club, which offers the conveniences of a small luxury hotel, guests are enjoying a cordial with a sparkling view toward the Intercoastal Waterway. Many others are retiring for the night. But at a large hotel like The Breakers, something is always happening. The Seafood Bar is busy. This upscale raw bar, whose two aquarium bars overlook the ocean, does not close until 1:00 a.m. The gala ball is also going strong. Waiters have cleared away the dinners, but they are still serving dessert, coffee, and after-dinner drinks. Dancers will crowd the ballroom floor until well after midnight.

11:30 p.m. Most of the activity at The Breakers after 11:00 p.m. prepares the hotel for the next day. About this time, for example, the hotel staff starts the heavy cleaning, particularly in the lobby, hallways, and "back-of-the-house" areas, so that everything is sparkling by early morning. In the kitchen the stewards put away the china and silver, empty out the steam tables, and remove the trash. Finally they use pressure cleaners to scrub down the floors, stainless-steel equipment, steam tables, and all the food preparation and serving areas.

12:00 a.m. In the hotel offices the night auditors work all night long, pulling together the figures for the day. It is a race against the clock. They must wait until all the restaurants and bars are closed and gather all bills. Then they have to prepare the statements for guests who will check out the next morning, some as early as 6:00 a.m.

1:00 a.m. The Breakers also has its own twenty-four-hour security force, which watches the security cameras posted around the property, patrols the grounds and outbuildings, and discreetly monitors the lobby and upstairs hallways. The security force also handles the hotel's lost-and-found department. Staff and guests find five thousand valuable items a year throughout the hotel and grounds, including boxes of new designer clothing, watches, cameras, children's toys, even bicycles. Guests lose the most amazing things at The Breakers. One housekeeper found $100,000 in cash in a room after a couple had checked out, while another discovered $75,000 worth of jewelry. A gardener retrieved a three-carat diamond ring in the Mediterranean Courtyard. One honeymooning couple checked

out, leaving the bride's wedding gown in the closet. They called several hours later, quite embarrassed, when they realized what they had done.

2:00 a.m. As guests sleep, the bakers arrive in the basement bake shop, one of the busiest places in the hotel at night. In a matter of hours bakers prepare fresh breakfast breads and pastries for the next morning. They also produce a wide variety of desserts, including cakes that will be frosted and decorated later in the day for the hotel restaurants and special events such as private birthday parties.

4:00 a.m. Four hours before a Fortune 100 company holds a meeting in the Flagler Board Room, a hotel staff member is already beginning the setup, organizing the table and chairs, ensuring that the audiovisual equipment is ready, arranging Breakers note pads and pens at each place, setting out water pitchers and glasses, placing dishes of candies on the table, and making sure that the room is spotless.

5:00 a.m. The office assistant opens the housekeeping department for the day. For the next two hours she prepares the day's work assignment lists on her computer. This is no easy task: the room attendants, housemen, and laundry workers number 210.

5:15 a.m. The twenty-four-hour room service department is fairly quiet now. But in about an hour the staff will begin to receive orders for as many as several hundred breakfasts to be cooked and served between 7:00 and 10:00 a.m. That means they must get ready now. One crew presets room service carts with china, silverware, napkins, and flowers. Another crew picks up fresh-baked breakfast breads and pastries at the hotel bakery, while a colleague prepares the butter plates. One attendant squeezes fresh orange juice, fills dozens of glasses, and then covers each glass with cellophane. Yet another cuts up fresh grapefruit, papaya, and melons into perfect slices and then arranges them onto plates, adding a garnish of fresh mint leaves.

5:30 a.m. Dozens of groundskeepers begin to spread out across the resort's parklike landscape. One crew starts by

Clockwise from top left: The Breakers provides all the comforts of home—and more—from breakfast in the News and Gourmet to one prepared by the chef, to elegant meeting places such as the Flagler Boardroom, and to luxurious oceanfront guest rooms.

cleaning up fallen leaves, newspapers, and other debris from the terraces and grounds and washing all walks, leaving the grounds immaculate. At 6:00 a.m. the greens are walk-mowed. A single gardener cares for the five hundred potted plants around the courtyards and grounds, watering, fertilizing, and trimming dead leaves. Others tend to the award-winning theme gardens while greeting guests out for their morning run. By midmorning some grounds-keepers switch to larger, noisier projects such as mowing the grass, edging, and weeding. Gardeners also tackle seasonal duties from planting annual flowers along the pathways (feeding 25,000 of them a year) to trimming the hedges and trees. Reverse osmosis water treatments and irrigation adjustments are made and recorded as part of the meticulous grounds care, which finally ends about 6:00 p.m.

5:45 a.m. The first members of the golf staff arrive at the Golf Clubhouse overlooking the Ocean Course. They study the tee sheets to determine how many golf carts will be needed that day and when and prepare for that morning's earliest players. The first tee time is 7:30 a.m., when the pro shop also opens.

6:00 a.m. The busy and efficient laundry department resumes its operations in the basement. The restaurant, pool, and spa linen, which was brought down overnight, is washed, spun damp, and then put through the large machine that dries and irons each item. By midmorning the crew finishes with the restaurant linens. Then it is time to start washing the guest room sheets, pillowcases, and towels, which are arriving as the room attendants clean the rooms. The laundry will not close until 11:00 p.m. On a busy day it washes and dries 16,000 pounds of linens.; over the course of a year the total is more than five million pounds. That is why the laundry needs thirty people on its staff. Even though The Breakers purchases high-quality linens, continuous heavy usage and daily washing soon wear them out. In a typical year the hotel spends $500,000 on new restaurant linen and guest room sheets, pillowcases, and towels. New towels for the Beach Club pools and Spa cost another $50,000.

6:45 a.m. "Good morning, Mr. Palmer. It is 6:45, and this is your wake-up call. Our forecast is for fine Florida weather in the 80s. You might like to know that Dobbs Ferry, New York [Mr. Palmer's hometown], is expecting a high of 31 degrees and snow. Have a wonderful day." On

sold-out days the telephone operators make approximately one hundred fifty wake-up calls. But these represent only a fraction of the hotel operators' duties. They typically take two thousand incoming calls every day, not including inquiries to the reservations line, the thousands of guest calls to numbers outside the hotel, and calls to various parts of the hotel and to friends in other rooms.

7:00 a.m. Early birds of both sexes are up and ready to pamper themselves at the Spa, recently voted one of the ten best hotel spas in the United States. After open-air tai chi on the ocean terrace and laps in the pool, one of the first guests arrives for her deep-cleansing, purifying facial. In the Spa's Tranquility Suite, cares float upward on the notes of Pachelbel's Canon. Another hour melts away during a tropical citrus wrap. And for dessert: an oceanfront massage in a secluded tent. Later, spa serenity continues over a healthful lunch at the Beach Club Restaurant.

7:15 a.m. Room attendants arrive at the housekeeping department and get their assignments for the day. When their shift begins at 8:00 a.m., they pick up their keys and carts, stocked overnight with cleaning supplies, fresh linens, bars of soap, miniature bottles of shampoo, and other toiletries. The Breakers goes through enormous quantities of these items a year—165,000 bars of soap, 68,000 bottles of shampoo, and 53,000 bottles of lotion. At 8:30 a.m. the room attendants start working in teams to service about twenty-four rooms a day. First they clean the vacant rooms whose occupants have already checked out, then they work on rooms where the guests are out.

7:45 a.m. Pool and beach attendants arrive for work at the Beach Club, a highlight for many guests. The attendants clean the area thoroughly, reset the chairs, and put out the towels. On a busy day more than one thousand persons will visit the pool and use three thousand towels. Cabana attendants also report for work, attending to the sixty-eight pool and oceanfront cabanas. Some cabanas are available to hotel guests by the day or for the length of their stay. Most are rented to club members on an annual basis. Some families have rented their own cabana season after season.

Left: At the Spa, tensions evaporate in the sea air, aided by the sound of the breakers. For the ultimate massage, guests are escorted to a luxurious tent that opens out to the ocean.

8:00 a.m. "Good morning. Room service. Sue speaking. May I help you?" Room service attendants take the guests' breakfast orders, quoting a delivery time of a half hour or less and repeating the order. As the cooks prepare hot dishes like eggs or French toast, attendants get the orange juice, fresh fruit, bread, and coffee. At the last minute they place the hot dishes in the warming box under the service carts. As a final step a supervisor confirms the order. Then the room service attendant heads for the service elevator. Within minutes, he or she arrives in one of the upstairs guest room hallways, picks up a telephone, calls the room, and announces that breakfast will be served momentarily.

9:00 a.m. After climbing out of their Breakers-issued sleeping bags, a ten-year-old boy and his seven-year-old sister are raring to go. They gleefully become members of the family-friendly hotel's Coconut Crew Interactive Camp (named after the resort's parrots) and set out for a day of swimming, snorkeling, tennis lessons, and a treasure hunt in the Secret Garden. The youngsters enjoy every minute of their time outdoors, thanks to ideas contributed by the Kids' Advisory Board. When it rains, movies, board games, and scavenger hunts are on the agenda indoors.

9:30 a.m. The loading dock is filled with deliveries of food and supplies for the kitchens at The Breakers. In a typical year the hotel purchases enormous quantities of food: 168,000 pounds of beef (much of it prime grade), 73,000 pounds of flour, 79,000 pounds of sugar, 54,000 pounds of butter, and 518,000 eggs. Despite these numbers, no item enters the hotel until it is inspected for quantity and weight as well as quality. Any delivery that does not meet the resort's specifications is sent back. Some of the most important and delectable ingredients are delivered in fairly small quantities: fresh fish caught just a few hours earlier, crab meat superior to what a home cook could find at the store, organically grown lettuces and baby vegetables, wild mushrooms, and fresh goat cheeses. The chefs work closely with local purveyors, supporting their small-scale enterprises and ensuring access to their best products. To get the freshest possible herbs, the chefs can gather them in the hotel's own herb garden right before meal preparation starts.

Clockwise from top left: Shoppers flock to The Breakers News and Gourmet for gourmet kitchen accessories, to the Piaget Shop for fine jewelry, to the Coconut Crew for kids' togs, and to Absolutely Suitable for the latest fashions in swimwear.

10:00 a.m. A room service attendant picks up a telephone and dials extension 8436—numerals that actually spell out THEO (Team Hears Every Opportunity). She leaves a voicemail message, one of some 2,000 comments a month The Breakers actively solicits from its staff to help the hotel quickly meet guest needs and answer any concerns. Measuring itself not merely against industry standards but against its own potential, The Breakers uses a similar computerized system to log preferences into a guest's history. To prepare for new arrivals, the resident manager and assistant manager confer daily, first reviewing reservations two days in advance and then again the day before arrival. Guest preferences are noted and every "i" dotted.

10:15 a.m. The hotel's security director meets with Secret Service agents to arrange a former president's visit to give a speech in the Gold Room, discussing how he will enter and leave the hotel. The Secret Service knows The Breakers well, because the hotel is accustomed to hosting presidents, royalty, and other heads of state.

10:30 a.m. The Signature Shop is filled with customers. Many guests want to take home Breakers-logo goods. In a typical year the Signature Shop sells 1,200 Breakers bathrobes, 7,200 sweat shirts, 12,500 baseball caps, 15,000 polo shirts, and more than 15,000 tee-shirts. Surrounding the Palm Courtyard are other boutiques selling enticing items from diamonds to crystal, clothing for adults and children, Guerlain cosmetics like those used in the Spa, private-label foods, gifts, books, and newspapers.

11:00 a.m. "Good morning. The Breakers Palm Beach. Room reservations. Mary speaking. How may I help you?" Every day more than six hundred calls stream into the hotel's reservations center. About eighty percent of the 250,000 annual guests—some of whom have surfed the resort's web site to get a digital preview—come from the United States. The remaining twenty percent are international visitors, with many arriving from Canada, Germany, Great Britain, Switzerland, and Latin America. A high percentage of guests are repeat visitors: 99 percent of them say that they will come back. As they pull up, returning guests are greeted like old friends and escorted to their rooms. Many families have been coming to The Breakers for generations and would not stay anywhere else. Who can blame them? This magnificent seaside resort continues to be irresistible after more than a century.

1830. Henry Morrison Flagler is born on January 2 in Hopewell, New York, near Canandaigua in the Finger Lakes region.

1844. Flagler leaves school at fourteen years to go to work.

1850. At the age of twenty Flagler becomes a grain commission merchant in Bellevue, Ohio. Shortly thereafter, he meets John D. Rockefeller, who is running a produce business in Cleveland.

1866. Flagler moves to Cleveland to work for Rockefeller's grain merchandising company. Rockefeller is devoting nearly all his time to the oil business. Flagler becomes involved in this company, named Rockefeller and Andrews.

1867. Rockefeller and Andrews becomes Rockefeller, Andrews and Flagler.

1870. The Standard Oil Company is incorporated. Flagler, a partner, soon becomes a multimillionaire.

1878. In March Flagler makes his first visit to St. Augustine, Florida, traveling with his wife, Mary, who suffers from tuberculosis.

1881. Mary Flagler dies on May 18.

1883. Flagler marries his second wife, Ida Alice Shourds, on June 5.

1883. The Flaglers arrive in St. Augustine in December for a vacation of several months.

1885. In February Flagler returns to St. Augustine, where he starts acquiring and developing property throughout the city.

1885. Flagler makes his first investment in a Florida railroad. In the coming years he purchases existing railroads and builds new ones, which are combined as the Florida East Coast Railway and enable travelers to reach his Florida resorts quickly and comfortably.

1888. Flagler's Ponce de Leon Hotel, the first luxury hotel built in Florida, opens in St. Augustine on January 10.

1889. Flagler builds the Alcazar Hotel near the Ponce de Leon.

1892. The Florida East Coast Railway is extended south to Daytona.

1893. Flagler announces plans to build his Florida East Coast Railway as far south as West Palm Beach.

1893. Flagler begins laying out the town of West Palm Beach.

1893. On May 1 Flagler starts construction of the Royal Poinciana Hotel on the eastern shore of Lake Worth.

1894. The Royal Poinciana opens on February 11 as Palm Beach's first luxury hotel, eventually becoming the largest hotel in the world for its day.

1894. The Florida East Coast Railway begins service to West Palm Beach on April 2.

1896. The Palm Beach Inn (later renamed The Breakers) opens on January 16 a half mile east of the Royal Poinciana Hotel, overlooking the ocean.

1896. Flagler extends the Florida East Coast Railway to Miami and opens the Royal Palm Hotel on Biscayne Bay.

1896. Flagler completes a bridge across Lake Worth in March so that the Florida East Coast Railway trains can take passengers directly to Palm Beach.

1901. The Palm Beach Inn is renamed The Breakers.

1901. On August 14 Flagler divorces his second wife, Ida Alice, who had been institutionalized several years earlier.

1901. Flagler marries his third wife, Mary Lily Kenan, in Kenansville, North Carolina, on August 24.

1902. In February the Flaglers move into Whitehall, their fifty-five-room mansion near the Royal Poinciana Hotel.

1903. The Breakers is destroyed by fire on June 9. Construction of a new, larger Breakers begins almost at once.

1904. The second Breakers opens on February 1.

1905. The American novelist Henry James visits The Breakers. In *The American Scene* (1907) he describes the hotel as "vast and cool and fair, friendly, breezy, shiny, swabbed and burnished like a royal yacht, really immaculate and delightful."

1905. In May Flagler starts construction of the Florida East Coast Railway between Miami and Key West. This section of his railroad line becomes known as the Key West Extension.

1912. Flagler arrives in Key West on January 22 for the official opening of the Key West Extension.

1913. Flagler dies on May 20 in a Breakers cottage at the age of eighty-three, after a fall at his nearby Whitehall. He is buried in St. Augustine.

1925. On March 18 The Breakers is completely destroyed in a spectacular fire whose smoke could be seen twenty miles away.

1925. The Turner Construction Company signs a contract to build the new Breakers on December 4.

1926. In January construction of the new Breakers begins in a rush to open just after Christmas 1926, the start of the Palm Beach season.

1926. The third (and current) Breakers opens its doors on December 29. This $7 million hotel was built in a record-breaking eleven months.

1926. The *Palm Beach Post-Times* hails The Breakers on December 30 as "a milestone in the architectural perfection of American hotels."

1927. *The Architectural Forum* in May praises The Breakers as "without doubt one of the most magnificent and successful examples of a palatial winter resort hotel."

1936. In February *Fortune* declares, "The new Breakers is undoubtedly the finest resort hotel in the world."

1942. Military personnel recuperate at The Breakers, renamed the U.S. Army's Ream General Hospital.

1942-44. More than a dozen babies—known as the "Breakers Babies"—are born at the hotel.

1944. In May the U.S. Army returns The Breakers to its owners, who prepare it for reopening.

1944. The Breakers reopens as a hotel on December 24.

1966. The Ocean Golf Clubhouse opens.

1969. The Breakers is expanded, gaining the Venetian Ballroom, extensive meeting facilities, and 150 new guest rooms. A new Beach Club replaces the older Beach Casino.

1970. Air conditioning is installed throughout the hotel.

1971. The Breakers remains open at the end of the traditional winter season, becoming a year-round resort.

1973. The landmark hotel is named to the National Register of Historic Places.

1995. A five-year renovation program is completed to launch the hotel's centennial year.

1996. The Breakers celebrates its centenary as a Palm Beach and national landmark.

1997-98. AAA awards its Five Diamond Award to the hotel, which soon earns ExxonMobil's Five-Star Award.

1999-2002. The Breakers marks a $130 million renaissance with its new Beach Club, Spa, and Golf Clubhouse; updated Ocean Course; and new Ponce de Leon Ballroom.